Bad
Chicks

LILLENAS DRAMA

Bad
Chicks

And Other Sketches and Monologues for Easter

By Larry & Annie Enscoe

Lillenas PUBLISHING COMPANY
KANSAS CITY, MO 64141

Questions? Please write or call:
    Lillenas Publishing Company
    Drama Resources
    P.O. Box 419527
    Kansas City, MO 64141
    Phone: 816-931-1900 • Fax: 816-412-8390
    E-mail: drama@lillenas.com
    Web: www.lillenas.com/drama

Cover art by Kevin Williamson

Contents

Dedication

To all the unsung heroes of church drama:
behind the curtain
behind the costumes
behind the sound and lights
behind the hammer, props, and paint
Without you, this book is just a book.

Bad Chicks

a sketch about grace

Cast:
SUSANNA: *20s*
ROBIN: *late teens, early 20s*

Costumes: Modern

Props:
Boxes of Easter chick "Peeps"
Gloves
Hairnets
Trash can

Running time: 5 to 6 minutes

Scene: A conveyor belt in the Cadberry Easter Chick Factory

Note:
This is a short comic sketch about grace. It can be used in youth groups or if you desire to offer something a little lighter during Easter. The conveyor belt action is all mimed. If you want, you can construct something to simulate the actual machinery.

(Sounds of a factory. Lights up on stacked boxes of yellow sugar Easter chicks on tables and a banner across stage that reads: "CADBERRY'S EASTER CHICKS." SUSANNA, *a young woman in her mid-20s, wearing hairnet and elbow-high plastic food gloves, stands at "conveyor belt." She watches yellow sugar Easter chick product come down the line, pulling out malformed or off-color chicks and throwing them into plastic-lined trash can. She is bored, low energy—Easter not her favorite holiday.* ROBIN *enters, wearing hairnet and plastic food gloves. She's been hired for the seasonal work and is very excited to be at the plant.)*

ROBIN: Are you Susanna?

SUSANNA *(drily, without looking up):* All day.

ROBIN: Oh, right. Yeah, so . . . they told me this is where the chicks hang out. (ROBIN *laughs.* SUSANNA *doesn't look up.)* OK, this is where I'm guessing you probably heard that one before, right?

SUSANNA *(sarcastically):* No, never. First time. The ironic mix of slang and seasonal humor was completely original.

ROBIN *(realizing what she's up against):* OK . . . uh, hi, I'm Robin. I started working here like 15 seconds ago and they said you're supposed to . . . take me under your wing. (SUSANNA *gives her a look.)* Oh, c'mon, that one rocked and you know it.

SUSANNA *(by rote):* Welcome to the Cadberry's family of Easter sugar products. Please listen to these instructions very carefully: The Quality Control Worker stands in

7

front of the conveyor system and watches the little yellow Easter chick products go by. If any of the aforementioned Easter chick products is less than perfect—either they aren't formed right or they're not just the right hue of chickie yellow—they get thrown in the Bad Chick Bin right here for disposal. Congratulations, now you know as much about this job as I do.

ROBIN: OK . . . well, how deformed? How off-color? I mean, is there some kind of Standard Cadberry Chickie Yellow I can look at and compare—?

SUSANNA *(holding up box of Easter chicks):* See the picture of the cute little chickie?

ROBIN: Which one? The one on the top of the box frolicking in the grass or the one hiding in the—?

SUSANNA: —Whatever!

ROBIN: OK. Yeah, I see the chickie.

SUSANNA: Good. So, they either look just like *that,* or they go in the Bad Chick Bin—

ROBIN: —for disposal. Got it.

(ROBIN *goes behind the conveyor belt. Sets box up in front of her for reference, starts watching chicks go by. Turns to watch* SUSANNA *expertly spot bad chicks, snatch them off the belt, and throw them in the Bad Chick Bin.* ROBIN *continues to watch the chicks go by; she smiles, grabs one, and throws it in bin.)*

SUSANNA: That one was good.

ROBIN: Sorry! *(Jumps to the bin to pull it out)*

SUSANNA: No! Leave it in there now!

ROBIN *(jumping back):* What?

SUSANNA: Leave it in there. Once it's in the Bad Bin, there's no going back.

ROBIN: What? That's not fair. Look, he's right there on top, just let me—

SUSANNA: Keep your eye on the chicks!

(ROBIN *jumps back to her place in line, watching chicks go by. After a moment . . .)*

SUSANNA: I think you should know you just cost Mr. Cadberry one and a half cents.

ROBIN: Said I was sorry.

SUSANNA: Just so you know.

ROBIN: Got it.

(ROBIN *sighs. They go back to checking chicks.* ROBIN *sees one she thinks is bad, reaches for it, decides it's good and stops, letting it go.* SUSANNA *snaps the chick off the belt and throws it in the bin.)*

ROBIN: C'mon, that one was *not* bad.

SUSANNA: That one was bad.

ROBIN: It was? How could you tell so fast?

SUSANNA: I've been doing this for five years.

ROBIN: Right. *(Smiles)* So I guess you could say these chicks are your "peeps."

(No laughter. ROBIN sighs, continues watching chicks, snags one and starts to throw it in the bin.)

SUSANNA: That one's good.

(ROBIN immediately turns to put the chick back on belt, but it's moving too fast and she can't get it back on. Impulsively she pops it in her mouth.)

SUSANNA: What are you doing?

ROBIN *(eating, makes face):* Oh, that is so nasty! It's almost pure sugar—

SUSANNA: Do you realize you just cost Mr. Cadberry—

ROBIN: . . . a penny and a half, I know. *(Chewing)* Oh, this is . . . do you have any idea how many carbohydrates must be in this thing?

SUSANNA: Seven.

ROBIN: Seven carbohydrates? There must be 100 carbos in this one chick. That's like two days' worth of carbos in one—

SUSANNA: No—seven bad chicks just went by while you were blabbing.

ROBIN: Oh, am I bad? Sorry.

(ROBIN goes back to checking the chicks. She grabs a bad one and throws it in bin, then misses one that SUSANNA gets. ROBIN is getting the rhythm of it now.)

ROBIN: Hey, did you ever see that classic "Lucy" episode where Ethel and Lucy are like watching these chocolate things go by, and it goes too fast and Lucy's all yom-yomyom, you know, stuffing chocolates in her mouth and the belt speeds up and Ethel starts yomyomyom, stuffing chocolate in *her* mouth and—

SUSANNA: I don't watch TV.

ROBIN: Of course you don't. If you did, you might actually laugh or something and that would probably end all life as we know it.

SUSANNA: Bad one!

ROBIN: Where?

SUSANNA: There, bad one! There!

ROBIN: That's not a bad one!

(SUSANNA snags the offensive chick and hurls it into bin.)

ROBIN: Oh, c'mon, his eye was like, just off a little on one side—

SUSANNA: In the yellow chick business you have to be brutal!

ROBIN: Are you telling me there's like . . . no grace at all.

SUSANNA: None.

ROBIN *(grabbing a chick):* You are the Weakest Chick. Good-bye! *(Throws it in bin)*

SUSANNA: Exactly.

ROBIN: Well, that's just lame.

SUSANNA: Look, chicks are either good or bad. There is no fuzzy middle chick ground.

ROBIN: Well, I'm not gonna do it. I believe in showing grace, so I'm letting . . . *(spies a bad chick)* that one go.

SUSANNA: No, you're not.

ROBIN *(folding her arms):* Oh, yes, I am.

SUSANNA: No, you're . . .

(SUSANNA *goes for the chick,* ROBIN *steps in, shielding the chick as it goes by* SUSANNA, *blocking her attempt to grab it.)*

SUSANNA: Move!

ROBIN: No! He's pardoned! Don't touch it!

SUSANNA: Get out of the way!

ROBIN: Uh-uh! Don't touch it! DON'T TOUCH THAT CHICKIE!

SUSANNA *(one more grab at it):* It's getting away!

ROBIN: You're free, chick! Run! RUN!

SUSANNA *(absolutely stunned):* I . . . can't believe you did that . . .

ROBIN: Did what? C'mon, I just gave him a little chickie reprieve.

SUSANNA: No, no, NO! There are two kinds of chicks in the world: good and bad. You let a bad one get through! He was bad! He didn't deserve to get through!

ROBIN: Of course he didn't. That's what grace is. I gave the little chickie grace, even though his beak was, y'know, a little tweaked kind of . . . that way.

SUSANNA *(having a meltdown):* NO! NO TWEAKED BEAKS! NO TWEAKED BEAKS! WE HAVE A POLICY OF ZERO TWEAKED-BEAK TOLERANCE!

ROBIN *(staring at her):* Girl, you are *waaay* too into this thing. I mean, what if I sent *you* down this conveyor belt thing and we had to choose good and bad on you? Where would you go, huh? Through those doors or into the disposal bin? (SUSANNA *stares at her. She's literally never thought this before. Clearly she has no idea where she'd go.)* That's what I thought. Well, all I can say is, I really hope there's someone standing here who has a little bit of grace when you come through.

(Pause)

SUSANNA: Me too.

Blackout

10

Getting Directions

a Palm Sunday sketch

Cast:
>PETER: *any age*
>JOHN: *younger than Peter*

Costumes: Modern or modified biblical

Props: None

Running time: 5 to 6 minutes

Scene: A city street

Note:
>PETER and JOHN are looking for the donkey Jesus has asked them to find. Along the way, they talk about where things are going for Jesus . . . and for them. This is a comic-serious look at our plans and God's—and how they often aren't going in the same direction.

(PETER *and* JOHN *walk up center aisle of sanctuary.*)

PETER: I think we go this way.

JOHN: Which way?

PETER: Up there. I think. Right up . . . (*Goes to the top of the aisle, looks around, frowns*) Here. (*Points*) Maybe if we go over—

JOHN: We're lost. (PETER *looks a him.*) Face it. We're lost.

PETER: We're not lost—

JOHN: Yes, we are. Jesus told us to come into downtown and look for a guy with a donkey, and we have no idea where downtown is! I'm telling you, we should just ask for directions.

PETER: I don't need directions—

JOHN: Macho Peter, can't ask for directions.

PETER: I *can* ask for directions, I just don't *want* to—

JOHN: Oh, no. Not you. You don't need anybody's help, do you? (*Beat*) Except that one time—

PETER: Don't—

JOHN: Then you needed help, didn't you?

PETER: Don't go there. I'm warning you, John.

JOHN: "Master, help me!"

PETER: Look, I never said I could walk on water, OK?

JOHN: My point exactly. You can't walk on water. So you certainly should have no trouble believing we're lost and ask for directions.

PETER: OK, fine. Who am I supposed to ask?

(They look around at the audience.)

JOHN: All these people sitting around here and you can't ask one of them where we are?

PETER: You want me to just walk up to someone here and ask?

JOHN: That's right.

PETER: Just say, "Hey, have you seen a donkey around here?"

JOHN: That's what I'm saying.

PETER: Fine.

(Looks around, playing "eenie meenie")

JOHN: Just pick someone.

PETER: I am.

JOHN: Pick someone. Anyone. Pick!

PETER *(chooses an audience member)*: Excuse me, do you know where I can find a donkey around here?" *(To JOHN)* See, he doesn't know!

JOHN: Forget it. Let's just keep walking.

(They keep walking toward the stage.)

PETER: I wish it wasn't a donkey, anyway.

JOHN: What?

PETER: I wish we were looking for a horse. I want Him to ride into town on a horse.

JOHN: He's not like that. A donkey is . . . closer to the people.

PETER: Yeah, but a horse makes a better impression. A stallion. A white stallion. Or a jet black one. It's more . . . popular, respected. You can't get respect on a donkey. A donkey is not an animal of respect.

JOHN: A donkey is what He asked us to find. He *wants* to ride a donkey.

PETER: Fine. It's just a horse would say more about the . . . direction we're going.

JOHN: And what direction do you think we're going, Peter?

PETER: You know, *up*.

JOHN: So, you think things are going up?

PETER: Absolutely. All up from here. Today, we have a parade. We all parade into the place. We own the city. By the end of the week, I bet Jesus is high on the horse.

JOHN: Donkey.

PETER: Whatever.

JOHN: How do you know *up* is the direction God wants things to go?

PETER: Because everything's going our way, John. It's a sign from heaven. Everything's going just the way we always thought it would.

JOHN: I hope so.

PETER: You wait, by the end of the week I bet Jesus is the toast of the town. (JOHN *nods in agreement.*) It's just . . .

JOHN: What?

PETER: Well, it's just—you know, if I was running the show, I'd do things completely different.

JOHN: Yeah? How would you do it?

PETER: First, I'd get a wagon, cover it with flowers, and have Jesus on it, waving to the crowd.

JOHN: OK. And then?

PETER: Then I'd get Him into the Temple, you know, to talk to all the business folks, start making friends. People with money could really help us in the long run. We need to get on their good side. Then, to top it all off . . . I'd throw some kind of grand finale. You know, like a big dinner party.

JOHN: A dinner party.

PETER: Yeah, something with class. Something that says we're here to stay. *(Beat)* Anyway, that's the direction I'd go, if I was running things. *(Looks off)* John, what is that over there?

JOHN *(peers off):* Looks like a donkey.

PETER: Absolutely. Let's go.

(PETER *starts off,* JOHN *grabs his arm.)*

JOHN: Wait a minute, I have to say this. I just . . . I just can't shake the feeling that things are *not* going, you know . . . Up.

PETER: What? John, you're crazy. We're heading into a very bright future, here.

JOHN: I don't know . . .

PETER: Trust me, by the end of the week, I bet everybody in town will be looking up to Jesus. *(Grabbing* JOHN's *arm)* C'mon, let's go see a man about a horse.

JOHN: Donkey.

PETER: Whatever.

(They rush off.)

Blackout

Passionate Voices

an Easter verse-drama on the Gospels, the Psalms, and Isaiah

Cast:
> VOICE ONE: *spoken offstage*
> VOICE TWO: *any age/gender*
> VOICE THREE: *any age/gender*
> VOICE FOUR: *any age/gender*

Costumes: Modern (black clothes)

Props: None

Running time: 5 minutes

Scene: At the cross

Note:
> This is a simple verse drama about the Crucifixion. It was designed to reveal the heartfelt emotion in the Word of God.

Production note:
> A sound effects tape with hammering and the sound of rain is needed.

(Music plays in darkness for a moment, then stops. Sound of hammering, three times, then laughter. Lights up on the sanctuary platform.)

VOICE TWO *(striding on to platform, laughing)*: So! You who said you were going to pull down the Temple and rebuild it in three days! Come down from the Cross and save yourself!

VOICE THREE *(striding on to platform)*: He "saved" others, but He can't even save himself! Let this Christ, let this King of Israel come down from the Cross so we can see and believe!

VOICE FOUR *(striding on to platform)*: "I am the Son of God!" That's what He said! Well, if He trusts in God, let God rescue Him from the Cross now—if God would even want Him!

ALL VOICES: SAVE YOURSELF!

(SFX: Thunder and rain. Lights dim. ACTORS/VOICES TWO, THREE, and FOUR run to the side of the stage, ducking out of the "rain.")

VOICE ONE *(offstage)*: Father . . . forgive them. They don't know . . . what they are doing.

(ACTORS/VOICES stop, turn, and look up at the "cross" center stage. VOICE FOUR turns and walks downstage center.)

VOICE FOUR: It was nine o'clock in the morning when they crucified Him. The written notice of the charge against Him read, "King of the Jews." They crucified two thieves with Him, one on His left, the other on His right.

(VOICE TWO *and* THREE *walk to either side of the "cross."*)

VOICE TWO: Surely, He held our grief. He carried our sorrow.

VOICE THREE: But we thought Him stricken! Attacked by God and afflicted!

VOICE TWO: But He was pierced through for our sins—
He was crushed for our transgressions!
His pain brought us peace!
By His beating, we are healed.

VOICE FOUR: By noon, darkness had fallen across the whole country.

VOICE THREE: DON'T LEAVE ME!

VOICE TWO: Trouble is near, and there's no one to help me!
Many bulls have surrounded me.
Strong bulls are circling me!
They throw open their mouth,
Like a hungry, roaring lion.

VOICE THREE: I'm poured out like water.

VOICE TWO: My bones are out of joint.

VOICE THREE: My heart is like wax.

VOICE TWO: It's melting inside me.

VOICE THREE: My strength has dried up.

VOICE ONE (*offstage*): I'm thirsty!

VOICE TWO: I'm like broken pottery.
My tongue has dried to the roof of my mouth!

VOICE ONE (*offstage*): I'M THIRSTY!

VOICE FOUR: There was a jar of wine vinegar standing there. Someone soaked a sponge in it and lifted it to His lips.

VOICE THREE: You! You have laid me in the dust of death!

VOICE ONE (*offstage*): My God . . .

VOICE THREE: Dogs are surrounding me!
Evil men are closing in on me!

VOICE ONE (*offstage*): WHY HAVE YOU ABANDONED ME?

VOICE THREE: They pierce my hands and feet!
I can count all my bones!

VOICE ONE (*offstage*): They look at me!

VOICE TWO: Stare at me!

VOICE THREE: Gloat at me!

VOICE TWO: They divide my garments between them!

VOICE THREE: And for my clothing they cast lots!

VOICE FOUR: Then Jesus cried out with a loud voice:

VOICE ONE *(offstage)*: IT IS FINISHED! *(Pause)* Father . . . into your hands . . . I commit My spirit.

VOICE FOUR: He breathed His last. *(Long pause)* When the centurion heard His voice, and saw how He died, he said, "I am certain this man . . . was the Son of God."

Blackout

Sword Fight

an Easter week drama

Cast:
> MAN 1: *teens or 20s*
> MAN 2: *30s or 40s*

Costumes: Modern or biblical

Props:
> Bottles
> Cloaks
> Litter
> A sword

Running time: 5 minutes

Scene: Garden of Gethsemane

Note:

This is a sketch that uses the backdrop of Gethsemane after Jesus has been arrested to look at our plans and God's plans. It examines what we do in our own strength, and what God does in His own power. It can be used anytime during Easter week.

Friday, 1:12 A.M.

(Darkness. SFX: Gregorian chants. Lights up on park or garden. Stage is littered with bottles, blankets, cloaks. There's obviously been a recent struggle.)

VOICE *(offstage):* No! Stop!

(MAN 1 runs in. He drops to his knees and looks at the audience.)

MAN 1: Please, I don't wanna die.

(MAN 2 runs in. He grabs a short sword he sees lying on ground. Comes at MAN 1.)

MAN 1: No—

MAN 2: You just stood there.

MAN 1: Don't do this!

MAN 2: You did nothing.

MAN 1: I *couldn't* do anything. Don't hurt me!

MAN 2 *(coming at him):* I don't wanna hurt you.

MAN 1: You don't?

MAN 2: I wanna *kill* you!

(MAN 2 *chases* MAN 1 *around the stage.*)

MAN 2: You did nothing! You miserable, pathetic, knock-kneed, lily-livered—

MAN 1: Whoever lives by the sword will die by the sword!

MAN 2: Where have I heard that before?

MAN 1: *He* said it. Two hours ago. To *you!*

(MAN 2 *stops, thinking.* MAN 1 *sees his opportunity and points at the audience.*)

MAN 1: And what about *them?*

MAN 2: What *about* them?

MAN 1: They sat there and watched the whole thing. They didn't do anything either.

MAN 2 *(looks at the audience, realizes):* That's *right.*

MAN 1: Did you hear a peep from them? No. They just sat out there in the darkness—

MAN 2 *(to audience):* —and watched the whole thing!

(MAN 2 *advances on the audience.* MAN 1 *grabs a bottle for a weapon and gets his back.*)

MAN 1: Look at 'em. Playing innocent. Big round eyes. "Oh, we didn't see anything!"

MAN 2: "Ohhh, don't blame *us*—"

MAN 1: "We're just the audience—"

MAN 2: "We're *supposed* to just watch!"

MAN 1: Well, an audience has other responsibilities.

MAN 2: Bigger obligations.

MAN 1: You think you can just sit there?

MAN 2: You think this has nothing to do with you?

MAN 1: You think just because you ran in here and threw coats over that entire row so you and your friends and your family could sit up real close that it absolves you from this?

(MAN 1 *and* MAN 2 *huddle, then peer out at the audience.*)

MAN 2: They're culpable.

MAN 1: They're involved.

MAN 2: They're criminal.

(Looking at each other)

MAN 1: They're unarmed!

(*They charge the audience, yelling. Suddenly,* MAN 2 *stops, yanking* MAN 1 *back.*)

MAN 2: There's too many of 'em.

MAN 1: Right.

MAN 2: Put down your weapon.

MAN 1: Right. *(Waiting)* There's nothing we can do. *(Puts down bottle)*

MAN 2: Hah!

(MAN 2 *chases* MAN 1 *around the stage again.)*

MAN 1: Agggh! *(Stops)* Wait a minute, you did the same thing!

MAN 2 *(stopping):* I did not.

MAN 1: Yes, you did. You did the same thing. You did nothing too!

MAN 2: I was waiting for you to do something.

MAN 1: You're kidding.

MAN 2: Didn't you see me looking at you out of the corner of my eye? I was watching you. Waiting for your cue.

MAN 1: So this is all really *my* fault?

MAN 2: Every last bit of it.

MAN 1: So, I should take the blame, is that it? Is that what you want? You want me to take the fall for what happened tonight?

MAN 2: Absolutely.

MAN 1: Oh, well, why didn't you say so?

MAN 2: Well, I—

MAN 1: Let's not stop there. How about if I take the blame for *everything?* Not just tonight, but last night. And the night before. And the night before that—

MAN 2: Now we're getting somewhere—

MAN 1: —and how about the weeks and months and years before that! Just *kill* me for everything bad that's ever happened—

MAN 2: Every bad thing that's been done and left undone—

MAN 1: Everything evil—since the beginning of time! All of it! Go ahead, get it out of your system. Punish *me!* Go ahead. *(Pause)* Go ahead.

MAN 2: I can't.

MAN 1: Why not?

MAN 2: There's too much.

MAN 1: Too much what?

MAN 2: Too much that's gone wrong.

(They drop their combative stances. Pause.)

MAN 2: How did it happen?

MAN 1: Did you hear Him? He told them not to touch us.

MAN 2: He said . . . "Take Me."

MAN 1: He saved *us*.

MAN 2: And so they took Him.

MAN 1: And we did nothing.

MAN 2: There were too many of 'em.

MAN 1: I guess . . . well, I guess you tried to stop them, didn't you? You gave it your best shot.

MAN 2 *(looking at sword):* No, I just swung blind.

MAN 1: But you got one of them.

MAN 2: It was just a flesh wound.

MAN 1: Then He healed it. Like it never happened.

MAN 2: I wanted to look good. I wanted to look brave.

MAN 1: You were brave.

MAN 2: No. I was just a man. *(Beat)* I was just a man like all the other men I know. At the most important moments in our lives—when people depend on us the most— we fall asleep. Just like we did when He asked us to stay awake with Him.

MAN 1: Then we wake up, confused, terrified by the noise of a battle right in front of us.

MAN 2: We're not in control, we're barely awake most of the time, anyway! So we just start slashing and hitting, all rage and no plan.

MAN 1: And when sleeping and hitting and raging don't work, we—

MAN 1 and 2: Run away.

MAN 1: Typical. *(Beat)* So what do we do now?

MAN 2: We listen. Wait for the right moment to help Him. Make up for what happened here. We find a way to break Him free and hide Him somewhere.

MAN 1: Find some hole in the ground for Him to hide in where nobody can find Him.

MAN 2: And we'll only let Him come out when we know it's safe.

MAN 1: When will that be?

MAN 2: What's today?

MAN 1: Friday.

MAN 2: Sunday. On Sunday we'll get Him out of the city, get Him somewhere safe.

MAN 1: Good plan. Let's go.

MAN 2: We'll try Caiaphas's house first.

MAN 1: OK.

MAN 2: We'll wait in the courtyard, see if we can see Him.

MAN 1: What if someone recognizes us?

MAN 2: We'll tell 'em who we are. Proud of it. We stand right up and say, "My name is Peter."

MAN 1: "My name is John."

MAN 2: Just like that. Let's go.

MAN 1: I'm with you.

(MAN 2 *stops, looks at the sword.*)

MAN 2: I wonder if that guy's mad at me. About cutting off his ear, I mean.

MAN 1: At least he's got a miracle to talk about.

MAN 2: Let's hope we all will.

(The two MEN run out.)

Blackout

Matching Shoes and Handbags

Cast:
> MOM: *in her 30s or 40s*
> SAMANTHA: *teenager*

Costumes: Modern

Props:
> Table
> Chairs
> Pattern books
> Patterns
> Dressmaker's dummy
> Fabric
> Sewing machine

Running time: 5 to 6 minutes

Scene: A front room

Note:
> This is a short sketch about finding your own relationship with God.

(Lights up on dining room table strewn with bolts of colorful fabric. Sewing machine is off to one side with dressmaker's dummy nearby. MOM and SAMANTHA enter, carrying two or three heavy pattern books. They dump the books on the table with a thud.)

SAMANTHA: Mom, I'm telling you this is a waste of time.

MOM: No, it's not. Look, all we have to do is flip quickly through spring of '68 and summer of '75.

(MOM starts flipping happily through one of the books. SAMANTHA stands there with her arms folded.)

SAMANTHA: I have to be at study group in an hour.

MOM: C'mon, Samantha. It'll go fast if we skip the polyester pantsuits and go straight to those cute wrap dresses.

SAMANTHA: Like that right there. *(Pointing at the page)* That's what I mean by a waste of time.

MOM *(looking at the page)*: Oh, I know. Fake fur. Gives me the shivers.

SAMANTHA *(sighs, exasperated)*: You just don't get it.

MOM: And I never will. Give me a nice 100 percent cotton any day—

SAMANTHA: Mom . . . *Mom!*

MOM: What?

SAMANTHA: This isn't going to work.

MOM: Yes, it will. C'mon, honey. Just one more year—

SAMANTHA: That's what you said last year—

MOM: I know. Then I found that super cute jumper pattern with the matching bandanas.

SAMANTHA: Super cute? We looked like Swiss Miss and Swiss Mrs.!

MOM: Oh, it wasn't that bad. *(She points to another pattern)* Look! We'd look great together in this one—

SAMANTHA: Mom. *(Reaching over to slam the book shut)* Every year since I was little you've made us matching Easter Sunday outfits—

MOM: No, you're wrong. If you remember, there was that one year. You were 7 . . . wait, no 8. I slipped on a scrap of taffeta and broke my arm. Couldn't sew a thing until Labor Day.

SAMANTHA: Well, you know, maybe it's time you took another break.

MOM: You're so sweet. But I don't need a break. Not from this, anyway. I look forward to sewing our matching Easter dresses all year. Hey, you know what? It was at last year's Easter brunch where I got the idea for this year's theme . . . *(Spoken like reading a headline)* Roses! I'm sure I told you this. Aunt Mary and I were doing the dishes and I scraped some leftover ham off one of my china plates—you know, the ones with the rose in the middle—and it hit me: "Up from the Grave He Arose!"

SAMANTHA: Uh . . . OK, you lost me.

MOM: Grave-he-a-rose. Grave-he. *Grav-y*. Up from the gravy a rose. Get it?

SAMANTHA: I'm afraid so.

MOM: So I thought, that's perfect. We'll do this, like, retro-rose print. Something simple, with a sweetheart neckline. *(Whips open pattern book)* Just a sec. I'll find it.

SAMANTHA: You can find it. But I won't wear it.

MOM *(looking at her)*: You're serious?

SAMANTHA: You have no idea how serious.

MOM: Oh. *(Closes the book)* Wow. Sorry, honey. I guess I haven't been listening.

SAMANTHA: No, you haven't.

MOM: OK. I hear you.

SAMANTHA: Finally.

MOM (*shoving pattern books to* SAMANTHA): You want to pick your *own* pattern.

SAMANTHA: What?

MOM: It's OK, Hon. You pick it. Whatever you want. This year I'll make us the Easter outfit *you* want to wear. Pattern, fabric, accessories. You can design it for both of us.

SAMANTHA: Mo-*ther*—

MOM: One request: no leather. I just can't wear leather in church.

SAMANTHA: STOP! (*to herself*) Calm down, Sam. Explain as you would to a child. (*She smiles at* MOM, *and slowly, gently closes the pattern book, and sets it aside.*) Mother, we need to talk. You know that scripture that says there's a time for everything? A time to laugh, a time to cry, and all that? That's what I'm trying to tell you.

MOM (*nods knowingly*): Oh, I get it. The rose theme. Too seasonal, huh?

SAMANTHA: Noooo. Not the rose theme. The mother-daughter theme. There was a time for matching shoes and handbags, Mom. And that time is over.

MOM: Oh, Sam, you don't—

SAMANTHA: Let me finish. I'm serious, Mom. I've thought about this a lot. (*Beat*) I'm not mini-you. I'm *me*. And I want to look like it. Even on Easter Sunday. I guess, especially on Easter Sunday.

MOM: Wow. OK.

SAMANTHA: It's just that at school lately I've been working hard at being an individual, making up my own mind about what I'm going to wear, what I'm going to do, who I'm going to hang out with. And then I come home and get more peer pressure from *you* than my friends!

MOM: I'm sorry, Sam—

SAMANTHA: No, it's OK. I just want to find out what I want. What I believe. I mean, I know it sounds crazy, but for so long I've even had your relationship with Jesus. Now, I want my own.

(*Silence while that sinks in*)

MOM: I'm glad you told me. That's what I want too. I mean, not what I want . . . I mean, I want it because you want it— OK, I'm going to shut up now and put this stuff away. (*Starts packing away supplies*)

SAMANTHA: Mom, don't do that yet.

MOM: I'm just moving the taffeta. It's a safety hazard.

SAMANTHA: I'm not finished.

MOM: Just don't you blame me for bellbottoms. You chose those yourself.

SAMANTHA (*grinning*): Right. What I was going to say is . . . Thank you.

MOM: For what?

SAMANTHA: For being the kind of mom who plans all year what she's going to make us for Easter. For being the greatest mom in the world.

(Beat)

MOM: Actually, I should really thank you.

SAMANTHA: For what?

MOM: For saving me.

SAMANTHA: From what?

MOM *(points at the pattern book):* From looking like a walking tablecloth. That rose idea was a real stinker.

(SAMANTHA *laughs.*)

Blackout

Spring Is Breaking Down All Over

a comic sketch about the "E" word

Cast:
    PIANO PLAYER: *any age/gender*
    DIRECTOR: *a woman of any age*
    PRINCIPAL: *a man of any age*
    CHOCOLATE BUNNY: *any age/gender*
    YELLOW CHICK: *any age/gender*
    COLORED EGG: *any age/gender*
    SPRING FLOWER: *any age/gender*
    (Kids' roles may be played by older children, teens, or adults.)

Costumes:
    Modern
    Bunny costume
    Chick costume
    Egg costume
    Flower costume

Props:
    Stage curtain
    Potted fake flowers
    Banner
    Signs

Running time: 8 to 10 minutes

Scene: A stage in an elementary school auditorium

Note:
    Using the school "Easter" pageant as a springboard, this sketch pokes fun at the lengths we'll go to keep God out of school. Also, how out of the mouths of babes . . .

(Piano music is heard in darkness—something light and snappy like what you'd hear at a children's pageant. Lights up as PIANO PLAYER comes to the end of the song. On-stage is a curtain and exaggerated fake spring flowers in pots downstage. A banner above the curtain reads, "MILLDALE ELEMENTARY'S FAMILY-SENSITIVE SPRING CAVALCADE." The DIRECTOR pokes her head around the curtain, sees the audience, and starts waving at the PIANO PLAYER to get his attention. She signals him to keep playing. PIANO PLAYER segues in to playing another snappy song while the DI-RECTOR drops back behind curtain. There is a lot of curtain wiggling and bumping from backstage. Someone begins feeling for an opening in the curtain, finally the

PRINCIPAL *steps out, dressed in garish spring colors. He is terrified. The* DIRECTOR *can be clearly seen in the wings encouraging him.)*

PRINCIPAL: Welcome, parents, families, and friends, to Milldale School's Family-Sensitive Spring Cavalcade. I'm the, uh, principal here at Milldale. *(Starts to loosen up)* Yes . . . and, uh, we're glad you're all here as we celebrate a time when life sprouts all around us and the *heavens* are *filled*—

DIRECTOR *(loudly from the wings):* Psssst!

*(*PRINCIPAL *looks at her as she holds up sign: it's the word "Heaven" with a red circle and slash through it.* PRINCIPAL *winces, looking back at audience, terrified again.)*

PRINCIPAL: Hoo-boy. Did I say heaven . . . ha-ha, uh, I meant, the *skies* are filled with . . . uh, birds and other flying . . . things. Uh, butterflies, right? And uh, moths and . . . stuff. *(Looks at* DIRECTOR *who gives him a thumbs up. He relaxes again.)* At this time of year, beautiful Easter eggs can be found hiding—

DIRECTOR *(loudly from wings):* AHEM!

*(*PRINCIPAL *looks to see her holding up sign: the word "Easter" with a red circle and slash through it.)*

PRINCIPAL *(sweating):* Whoa, wow, uh . . . did I just say, Easter? Yikes, sorry, I mean, fancy multicolored shelled embryos can be found hiding in the grass for children to, uh, find. *(Coughs and adjusts tie)* OK, moving on. So, directing this year's caval- cade, our school is *blessed* to have (DIRECTOR *makes strangulated "cut" sound)*— boy, ouch, sorry, not blessed, actually—we're really, really lucky to have our very own artsy type person, third grade teacher, Ms. Godwin—whoops, I didn't mean to say God. I am so sorry. Wait. That's her name. That's OK, then. Right. *(Pulls out handkerchief to mop forehead)* OK, take it away, Ms. Godwin!

*(*PIANO PLAYER *launches into some intro music as the* DIRECTOR *bounces onto stage. The* PRINCIPAL *takes a seat in the front row.)*

DIRECTOR: Hello, everybody! Happy Springtime to all of you! The kids have worked very hard, so let's get right to the fun. Oh, yes, and please—if anything we do tonight offends you in any way, please feel free to fill out the complaint form we've includ- ed in the program and we'll make sure the appropriate but sensitive steps are taken to remove it from next year's program. OK! Let's start the show!

(She signals to PIANO PLAYER *who plays jaunty, hopping-down-the-bunny-trail tune.* DIRECTOR *bounces down to sit with the* PRINCIPAL *where she will direct and coach the children. Curtain opens—nothing. We hear whispers. Someone is too scared to come out, then the first kid pops out onstage dressed like a* CHOCOLATE BUNNY. *Freezes at sight of audience.* DIRECTOR *waves him down front.* BUNNY *takes one step at a time, finally making it to stage apron. Says nothing.)*

DIRECTOR *(prompting):* I'm Hoppy—

CHOCOLATE BUNNY: Hoppy . . . I'm Hoppy the Springtime Bunny. Sometimes you can see me in stores and sometimes in Easter—

DIRECTOR: Spring—

CHOCOLATE BUNNY: Spring. Baskets. Filled with sweets . . . *(watching* DIRECTOR *mouth something)* in appropriate amounts. I am sugar-free, dairy-free, and made with soy butter. Hoppy says, don't forget to brush and floss and . . .

DIRECTOR: Run—

CHOCOLATE BUNNY: Don't run with—

DIRECTOR: Water?

CHOCOLATE BUNNY: Don't run with water? *(Getting it)* Don't let the water run. Thank you.

(CHOCOLATE BUNNY bows and moves to position upstage. Music plays again. The curtain opens and a kid dressed like a YELLOW CHICK comes running downstage flapping wings, obviously very comfortable onstage.)

YELLOW CHICK: I'm the Yellow Chick who likes to run around on the free range and eat Oregon seeds—

DIRECTOR *(correcting): Organic.*

YELLOW CHICK: Organic seeds. I am very happy on the farm, so please don't take me home for a pet, because I'll turn into a chicken and I don't want to be dinner!

(YELLOW CHICK runs back upstage. Music plays, curtain opens and a kid dressed like a COLORED EGG runs downstage.)

COLORED EGG: Hi, I'm a many-colored spring egg and I represent new life that *springs* out in so many colors! I can be very pretty and tasty, but be careful. Don't eat too many of me. Just three to five a week! Thank you!

DIRECTOR *(delighted):* Perfect!

(The COLORED EGG runs upstage, joining the CHICK and BUNNY. Music plays, curtain opens and a kid dressed like a SPRING FLOWER comes hesitantly downstage to apron.)

SPRING FLOWER: Hi, I'm a beautiful spring flower. I was a seed who sprung out of the ground because of all the rain that was . . .

DIRECTOR *(prompting):* Sent . . .

SPRING FLOWER: Sent.

DIRECTOR: From . . .

SPRING FLOWER: From.

DIRECTOR: The sky.

SPRING FLOWER: God.

(Music stops. All the kids look at the crazy FLOWER. The DIRECTOR looks like she might have a stroke.)

DIRECTOR: You mean the *sky.*

SPRING FLOWER: The sky doesn't send rain. God sends rain, silly.

DIRECTOR *(nervous):* Not in school, He doesn't.

SPRING FLOWER: Of course not in school!

DIRECTOR *(relieved):* That's right—

SPRING FLOWER: 'Cause school's indoors! God sends the rain outdoors because that's how God makes flowers!

DIRECTOR: Stop saying God!

SPRING FLOWER: You just said God.

DIRECTOR: I did not.

PRINCIPAL: Yes, you did. I heard you. You said, God.

CHOCOLATE BUNNY: Know what? I think God made chocolate. For the chocolate bunnies.

(The DIRECTOR turns to the PRINCIPAL.)

DIRECTOR: Now look what you've done! They're all saying it!

(Suddenly the YELLOW CHICK pops her head between them.)

YELLOW CHICK: God made rain and flowers and chocolate . . . and chicks!

COLORED EGG: I think God made the egg first, 'cuz chicks come from eggs.

DIRECTOR: Stop it! Stop it!

CHOCOLATE BUNNY *(tugging on PRINCIPAL's sleeve):* If God made rain and flowers and chicks and eggs, did He make me?

DIRECTOR *(to PRINCIPAL):* Don't answer that question!

PRINCIPAL *(sweating):* Uh . . . Hey! I have an idea. Let's sing a song to spring, shall we?

(FLOWER, BUNNY, CHICK, *and* EGG *launch into "Jesus Loves Me."*)

DIRECTOR *(slumping into seat):* I give up!

(The kids tromp offstage, voices fading as they disappear behind the curtain. The PRINCIPAL goes to the DIRECTOR holding his hand out to her. She takes it and gets wearily to her feet.)

DIRECTOR: I tried. I did.

PRINCIPAL: You did your best.

DIRECTOR: From the mouths of babes!

(They sigh.)

DIRECTOR: Are we going to do this again next year?

PRINCIPAL: I pray not.

DIRECTOR: Ah-ah. No prayer in school.

Blackout

Martha Stewart's Eternal Living

a sketch on real life

Cast:
> MAGGIE: *in her mid 20s*
> CHRIS: *in his mid 20s*

Costumes: Modern

Props:
> Dining table
> Chairs
> TV with VCR
> Videotapes
> Candles
> Candleholders
> Table settings
> Chocolate Easter tomb
> Small stone
> Goggles
> Oven mitts
> Platter
> Fake burnt lamb
> Mold

Running time: 6 to 8 minutes

Scene: A young couple's dining room

Note:
This is a short comic scene on trying to make Easter a perfect day—a hard act to follow since it was made perfect 2000 years ago. The humor is based on the Martha Stewart you-can-make-this-yourself "Living" programs and magazines.

(Lights up on a dining room. MAGGIE is at the dining table trying to get candles to fit into candlesticks. The table is formally dressed with six chairs. Each place setting has a small blob of chocolate sitting beside it. Nearby is a small table with TV/VCR. The floor around table is covered with videocassettes, labeled with titles and dates: "Martha Stewart—Beeswax Candles Episode 7/13"; "Martha Stewart—Silverware Episode 10/22"; "Martha Stewart—Easter Brunch Episode 3/10." MAGGIE can't get the candle bottoms to fit into the holders. Her anxiety is building.)

MAGGIE: C'mon . . . don't do this to me now. Martha Stewart's candles fit! Her candles always fit! Why am I such a *loser?*

(Suddenly, CHRIS rushes in wearing huge oven mitts and welder's goggles, seriously about to lose his mind.)

CHRIS: I can't do it!

MAGGIE: What do you mean, you can't do it?

CHRIS: I mean, I can't do it! Nobody can do it! Because it can't be done!

MAGGIE: Martha Stewart did it—

CHRIS *(yanking down goggles)*: I don't *care* what Martha Stewart did. You cannot smelt your own silverware over the kitchen stove using old tuna cans.

MAGGIE: Chris, you have to do it. This is our first Easter brunch as a married couple. It has to be perfect. My parents *and* your parents are going to be here in like . . . *(checking her watch)* 10 minutes! *(She grabs videotape, holds it out to him)* Watch Martha's smelting technique again. Maybe there's something you missed.

CHRIS: The only thing I've missed is 48 hours of sleep and the Easter service because you got all obsessed about copying some Mother of all Brunches you saw in some magazine.

MAGGIE: Chris, I'm surprised at you. Where's your Easter spirit?

CHRIS: Where's my Easter spirit? I don't know, Maggie. Maybe I missed that episode. Maybe you've got it on tape. Here it is! *(He grabs a tape with his mitt.)* It's called "Easter's dead 'cause Martha killed it!" *(He tosses the tape, yanks off his mitts.)* That's it. I'm done smelting.

MAGGIE: Sweetheart—

CHRIS: No.

MAGGIE: Honeybunch—

CHRIS: Forget it.

MAGGIE: That means we have to eat with our yucky old stuff.

CHRIS: What's wrong with our old yucky stuff? We eat with our old yucky stuff *every* day!

MAGGIE *(losing it)*: That's the point! It's everyday stuff. This is a special day. I've been planning it all *year.* I taped 37 episodes of Martha Stewart and watched each one nine times. I grew the Easter lilies with mulch I ordered directly from Jerusalem. I wove the place mats from the fronds of palm trees I climbed *myself.* I kiln-dried dishes, embroidered napkins, and airbrushed jelly beans— *(Grabs a small blob of chocolate from table)* Look! Easter tomb place card holders! For three days I covered gauze strips with organic chocolate! Each one has a tiny rollaway stone I made out of that little ball of cotton at the top of aspirin bottles!

CHRIS: Please don't tell me you shot and stuffed the lamb that's cooking in there.

MAGGIE: No, of course not. *(Beat)* I went out to the farm and hand-fed it.

CHRIS: You've got to be kidding.

MAGGIE *(about to cry)*: I'm doing everything I can to make this day perfect. The least you can do is go back in there and smelt!

CHRIS *(sighing)*: Whatever. Fine. I'm smelting. *(He watches* MAGGIE *go back to work on candles. He softens.)* Those the candles you made from beeswax?

MAGGIE: *Raw* beeswax.

CHRIS: Oh, yeah. So how are those beestings doing?

MAGGIE *(scratching)*: They stopped bleeding.

CHRIS: You know, you can buy beeswax in the store.

MAGGIE: That would be cheating.

CHRIS: Of course it would.

(He pulls on the goggles and exits. MAGGIE *continues to struggle with the candles for a moment, then grabs a knife to shave the candle bottoms.)*

MAGGIE: Martha, forgive me. *(SFX: Boom from offstage)* Chris!

CHRIS *(offstage)*: I'm all right!

MAGGIE: What happened?

CHRIS *(offstage)*: I think I just melted my smelter.

MAGGIE: Just . . . deal with it.

CHRIS: Dealing.

MAGGIE *(checks her watch, then looks at the room in a panic)*: I'm forgetting something . . . I'm forgetting someth—oh man! The organic Tuscan herbs I'm growing in the backyard!

*(*MAGGIE *exits. Silence.)*

CHRIS *(offstage)*: Uh . . . Maggie? Maggie? Sweetie? Uh, do you know where the fire extinguisher is? Baby? MAGGIE? *(Hear clanking and crashing)* OK! Uh . . . where's the baking soda? OK—wait, I found it. *(More crashing)* OK, the fire's out!

*(*CHRIS *runs in with blackened goggles askew on his head. He's carrying a platter with a charred black lump in his oven mitt hands.)*

CHRIS: Maggie? I'm OK! But the uh . . . the lamb didn't make it. Maggie? Where are you?

(He crashes into the table smashing everything, lamb, table, dishes, to the floor. He freezes. He yanks off the mitts and the goggles; staring at the disaster.)

CHRIS: Oh no . . . oh, dude, I'm so dead. She's gonna kill me and bury me in a coffin she made from used corn dog sticks!

*(*CHRIS *drops to his knees to pick up the mess.* MAGGIE *enters with bunch of greens in her hands, freezes, and lets out a small cry.* CHRIS *looks up at her.)*

CHRIS: OK, I can explain. The lamb was burning and I tried to save it, but my goggles melted and I ran into the table and . . . *(Holding up his hands)* HAVE MERCY!

MAGGIE: What . . . am I . . . going to do . . . ?

CHRIS *(setting table up and trying desperately to reset it):* I'll just glue these dishes to-gether. Quick, pop in that tape called "Making Fine China from Scrap." Our parents will never know the difference. Just give me five minutes— *(SFX: Doorbell. They pause, looking at each other.)* OK, plan B. We'll just tell 'em . . . uh . . . Martha Stewart's evil twin smashed everything. You know, trying to ruin her sister's career. *(SFX: Doorbell)* OK, Plan C. Denny's. They have some Fruity Rooty Easter Tooty.

(SFX: Doorbell. MAGGIE reaches down to pick up one small chocolate blob.)

CHRIS: OK, so the tomb. It looks OK.

MAGGIE *(a small smile begins to grow):* The stone in front. It's gone.

CHRIS *(desperately looking around the floor):* I can find that—

MAGGIE: No.

CHRIS: Wait, it's no problem. *(He grabs MAGGIE's hands, still holding the chocolate "tomb.")* Honey, I'll find the stone. It just . . . rolled away.

MAGGIE *(smiling):* You're right.

CHRIS *(looking up at her):* I am?

MAGGIE *(holding up tomb):* It's perfect.

CHRIS: What is?

MAGGIE: Easter. It's already perfect.

(SFX: Doorbell.)

Blackout

There

3 monologues for women on Easter week

Cast:
    SERVANT GIRL: *a teenager*
    MARY: *an older woman*
    MARY MAGDALENE: *a woman in late 20s to 40s*

Costumes: Modern or modified biblical

Props:
    Walkman
    Soda
    Crown of thorns

Running time: Each monologue 3 to 4 minutes

Scene: A mall food court, Golgotha, and the Garden tomb

Note:
In "Servant Girl" you can let the audience hear the music she's listening to at the beginning of the monologue and at the end.

"Magdalene" was written to come at the end of an Easter sermon or talk, seamless moving from spoken word to performed word.

The Servant Girl
based on Mark 14:66-72

(SERVANT GIRL *comes in, dressed in a fast-food restaurant uniform, drinking a Coke and listening to her Walkman. She nods her head to beat, then sees the audience and pulls the headphones off.*)

I work down here in the courtyard. It's a stupid job, but—anyways, that's where I seen 'im. Peter. That's his name, right? He's trying to get warm over there at the grill. He looks all fried. I'm starin' at 'im really hard. Starin' right at 'im. "You were with that Jesus, the guy from Nazareth, right?" But he totally denies it. He goes, "Don't know 'im at all. Got no idea what you're even talking about." And he walks away. You know, so, whatever—but I'm sure it's him, so I start asking some of the customers around. And I finally say, "Oh yeah. You're him. Don't even try to deny it." But he totally fronts me again. Right to my face. Then one of the other customers chimes in, "I know you're one of those disciples, bud. You're a Galilean." And this Peter guy goes completely off the hook. Starts cussin' at us. "I swear to God I don't even know who you're talkin' about!"

Then this rooster crows. And the guy turns totally white. Like somethin' freaked him out. And he starts babblin' about denyin' someone. Anyways, it was very bizarre. Then the guy starts cryin'. Right there. Covered his face and bawled like a baby. (*Pause*) Don't know why I should care, but it kinda made me feel sad for him.

(*She pulls headphones back on, nodding to the beat.*)

Blackout

Mary
based on Mark 15:33-41

(MARY *pulls a tattered sweater around her. It's cold. She sees something on the ground, and bends to pick it up. It's the crown of thorns. She covers her mouth to stop a cry.)*

It was noon when the world turned black. Three hours later, my Son cried out in a loud voice . . . "My God! My God, why have you forgotten me?"

(The emotion catches her. She takes a deep breath)

I heard someone near me say, "Did you hear that? He's calling Elijah." Somebody ran and soaked a sponge in sour wine, stuck it on a stick, and held it up for my Son to drink. "Let's see if Elijah comes to take Him down," the man next to me kept saying. Then . . . then my Son cried out once more. I heard His breath . . . His last breath. *(Beat)* I remember the officer . . . the officer looking up at Him. He heard my Son's cry and saw how He died. The officer said, "I am certain this man . . . was the Son of God."

(Beat)

They . . . they took a linen cloth and wrapped His body. They laid Him in a tomb. Then they rolled a stone over the entrance. It was sunset.

(Pause. Next words almost whispered.)

Shhh. Rest quietly, Child. Sabbath has begun.

Blackout

Mary Magdalene
based on John 20:13-18

(As the speaker or pastor is finishing, a woman comes out of the shadows from the back of the room. This is MARY MAGDALENE. *She walks slowly up the center aisle, crying softly. The speaker notices her. He watches for a moment, then . . .)*

SPEAKER: Excuse me . . . can I help you?

(MARY MAGDALENE *says nothing.)*

SPEAKER: Are you all right?

MARY MAGDALENE: I . . . I'm looking for someone . . .

SPEAKER: Why are you crying?

MARY MAGDALENE *(explodes):* They've taken away my Lord! I don't know where they've . . . put Him!

SPEAKER *(to the audience):* Then Mary Magdalene turned around and saw Jesus standing there. But she didn't realize it. He said:

MARY MAGDALENE *(taking over the narrative, turns to the audience):* "Why are you crying? Who is it you are looking for?" (SPEAKER *steps back out of the scene.)* I didn't know who this person was. I thought He was the gardener. "Sir . . . please, if you've taken Him away somewhere, tell me where He is and I'll go get Him."
    Then He said one word to me: "Mary." I turned toward Him. I looked Him in the face. The voice. My name. That face. It was Him. "Rabbi!" I fell on the ground. I was going to touch His feet, but He stepped back. "Don't hold onto me. I haven't returned to my Father. Go to my brothers and tell them, 'I am returning to my Father and your Father, to my God and your God.'"

(Pause)

    That's what I did. I ran to the disciples with the news. I told them everything I knew. Everything He said to me. *(She starts down the aisle.)* "He's returning to . . . His Father. Our Father . . . Our God."

(She breaks into a run . . .)

    I've seen Him! Peter! John! Mary! Salome! I've seen Him! It was Him! It IS HIM! *(Beat)* I'VE SEEN THE LORD!

Blackout

I Should Live So Long

a monologue on dying

Cast:
ROBERT: *an older man*

Costume: Modern

Props:
Table
Chair
Healthy breakfast food
Newspaper

Scene: A kitchen table at breakfast

Running time: 5 to 6 minutes

Note:
This is a light but very serious look at being afraid of death. It is meant as evangelism for Easter or anytime.

(Lights up on ROBERT sitting at a kitchen table. Healthy breakfast foods are in front of him: granola, salt-free peanut butter, etc. He's reading a newspaper. He looks up at audience, and holds up paper so it can be seen.)

Section B, page 4. The obits. I always end up on the same page every morning. Every morning I wake up and tell myself, "Robert, read the front page first this time, OK? Or maybe, how about the sports section this time." But nope, I turn right to the obits. I don't know, it's—well, it's like that old joke. Those of you . . . how can I say this? . . . Those of you of a certain *age* have probably heard this one before. It goes like this: You know it's gonna be a good day if you turn to the obits page and you're not on it.

(Winces)

OK, that was . . . I'm not a good joke teller anymore. You know, like that uh, Benny . . . I forget his name . . . uh, Green. No, Shecky, uh . . .

(Gives up)

I'm telling you, my memory is so . . . You know, they say memory is the second thing to go. The first thing to go is your ability to tell jokes. Wait, no, . . . um, memory is the second thing to go, the first to go is . . . uh . . . I forget.

(He looks back at paper, then at the audience.)

OK, wait, this is what I'm really trying to say: laughter is the best medicine. Laughter is actually supposed to prolong life. Trouble is, the older you get, the less there is to laugh about.

(Shows the paper)

OK, now this guy. 83 years old. He went after a lengthy battle with some undisclosed illness, right? C'mon, isn't that what you'd expect from 83? Nope, this guy goes out by getting hit by a car. And he was riding a bike! 83 years old. Now that's the way you should go, huh? Rounding third, heading for home, right? That's the way it should happen. That's the way I wanna go.

(Pause)

Actually, that's a lie. That's not the way I wanna go out. I don't want to go out at all.

OK, wait—now I know that sounds pretty egotistical. But what I mean is, I *know* I have to go sometime, but I *wish* I didn't have to go. And you know what? There's no reason I should have to go, right? I mean, not anytime soon. Aren't they making advances *every* day in medicine and in prolonging . . . no, I mean, in longevity.

(He puts his glasses on and starts pointing to food on the table)

And I'm absolutely doing everything I can to keep myself around. Absolutely. Look at this. This granola product I'm eating here. There are 57 kinds of grains in this thing. I didn't even know we had 57 kinds of grains on the planet. They've even got some stuff in here the ancient Egyptians ate. Kaput or something. And one grain can only be found under the Amazon basin. Under a full moon. And there's uh . . . there's something like 7 kinds of seaweed and . . . 4 kinds of twigs . . . 3 kinds of dirt, and a whole slough of vitamins and amino acids. And look, they've *even* got a pinecone in here. *(Looks at audience and smiles)* 'Cuz, you know, many parts are edible. *(Laughs)*

OK, does anybody get that joke anymore? Euell Gibbons. Anyone? Anyone? "Many parts are edible." *(He sighs.)* Oh man, don't you just hate that? Don't you hate it when you've lived long enough that nobody gets the joke anymore. I tell you what, someday one of you is going to make a joke about Britney Spears and everybody is going to stare at you with "who?" written all over their smug little faces. You wait, it'll happen. I should live so long to see *that.*

(Moving on) OK, and over here, I've got some salt-free peanut butter made with organic peanuts with the oil on top for which you need an arm like Steve Reeves to actually mix up. And this—for on my organic 9 grain, 6 legume toast—here we have soy butter. Tofutter. I mean, it's . . . it tastes like . . . well, about as good as cereal made with twigs and seaweed, so there you go. But they say, every time you spread this on your toast, you add 15-point-2 minutes to your life.

So, you see, I'm doing all I can. Of course, the stress of craving two eggs over and some Jimmy Dean pork sausage is probably putting a bigger strain on my heart than a big scoop of Land O'Lakes, but . . . what're you gonna do?

I mean, I really wanna stick around a long time. I want to see them put someone on Mars. Really. I really do. And I wanna see a hotel in space. And I wanna see if Charo can really make a comeback. Oh, don't tell me you don't know who Charo is? What's this world coming to? *(Sighs)*

Look, before you think I'm some big coward, I should say I'm not afraid of dying. I mean, who wants to die, but I'm not afraid of it. No, . . . really, it's not dying that scares me. It's death. Death is what scares me.

(The thought of that sinks in for a moment. Then he shakes it off.)

But, you can't tell people that, right? It wigs them out. It gives them the willies. "Hi there, are you as afraid of death as I am?" "No, not me, I love life! I'm high on life!" Or then you get the person who says, "No, I'm not afraid of death. I know where I'm going." Those people just . . . I don't know. I mean, they really believe they know where they're going. That just burns me up!

(Checking pulse) Look at me. My pulse is sky-high. Some coffee and a Danish and I might reach my target heart rate.

(He lets out a calming breath.) OK, look, I don't want to be a downer, so . . . forget I got into all that morbid, ghosty woo-woo where-do-we-all-go-after-death stuff. Let's just concentrate on the here and now. I mean, the point is, they're making huge advances in medicine every day, right? New hearts, new livers, new . . . everything. So, why should I worry about this stuff now? I mean, I plan to be here a long, long time.

(He picks up a box off the table.)

Did you know they can make bacon out of tree bark?

Blackout

No Comin' Back

a monologue on suicide

Cast:
>BRIAN: *15- or 16-year-old young man*
>MAN: *Brian's dad, 30s to 50s*
>BRIAN'S MOM: *offstage voice*

Costumes: Modern

Props:
>Discman
>Discman/CD case
>Boxes
>Bible
>Old clothes
>Old dishes
>Metal cash box
>Handgun

Scene: An attic

Running time: 5 to 6 minutes

Note:
>This is a very serious monologue on suicide. It was written to be used only with discussion or teaching to follow. It is designed to be real, no pat answers. It doesn't sugar-coat the subject.

(Scene opens in darkness. Hear some speed metal music for a moment. Then it slows and stops. Lights up in an attic filled with boxes. A young skater-looking boy, BRIAN, is digging through boxes, listening to his Discman. He realizes the music stopped because the Discman batteries died. BRIAN whips the headphones off. He looks at the Discman, punching buttons. His fingernails are painted black.)

BRIAN: Great, the stupid thing's dead. Whatever, just like everything else, right? *(Opens Discman and pulls the dead batteries out. Looks in the Discman case for more batteries.)* Hello. Batteries. Oh, c'mon . . .
>*(Can't find batteries, flings the old ones into an open box)* Yeah, OK, whatever. Just like my life. What I need, nobody's got.

(He continues digging in boxes, not finding what he's looking for. He pulls over another box. It's labeled "old dishes." He opens it and starts taking dishes out, setting them aside.)

>Let me just say, straight up, before any of you guys think you nailed me, like, who I am. What kinda kid I am and like that. I'm not one of those whiner guys, thinkin' the world owes me whatever, y'know, just 'cuz I was born. Yeah, and I'm not one of those morose Goth spookies, those guys who, like, slice their girlfriends'

names into their arms and stuff and OD on death metal. And I'm not a card-carrying member of the trenchcoat mafia, either. Although me and my boys get some smack from the straights sometimes—you know who I'm talkin' about, those guys *(in straight radio voice)* "Most Likely to Succeed." And I've had to, y'know, power down on a couple for which I *always* take the heat. But that's life, right? I mean, what's fun about growin' up if you can't find somebody different than you and throw down on 'em? That ain't gonna change. Maybe whoever's comin' up now can change that, but I seriously doubt it.

(He doesn't find what he wants in boxes, so he throws the dishes back in. He closes the box up and shoves it away. Reaches for another box . . .)

BRIAN'S MOM *(offstage)*: Brian?

*(*BRIAN *jumps up, running to a light switch to "turn off" lights. Stage goes black.)*

BRIAN'S MOM: Brian? Are you up in the attic? Brian? I'm going to the store. Bye, sweetheart.

(Door slams, then silence. Stage lights back up as BRIAN *"turns on" the light.* BRIAN *walks back to boxes. Now there's a* MAN *sitting there. He's wearing a slightly rumpled suit and a crooked tie.* BRIAN *doesn't even notice he's there.)*

BRIAN: If my mom knew I was up here, she'd freak. So it's better if she goes to the store and stuff. (MAN *smiles and nods.* BRIAN *still doesn't notice him, opens another box and looks through it.)* Why is nothin' around when you need it?

(He shoves the box aside, grabs one marked "Dad's stuff." Opens it and looks inside, pulling out old clothes, photos, and some albums. The MAN *watches his every move.)*

Y'know, I guess I'm not a stress or a freak to anybody. Except myself. And that's the problem. See, 'cuz there's all this talk about gettin' to know who you are, and I feel like I know who I am and I don't like me. Whatever. The world's hard, right? So, the question is, if I don't like this round, y'know, what I got on this deal, do I get to come back? My dad didn't like what he got, so he checked out and didn't come back.

*(*MAN *slumps at that.* BRIAN *finds a book. He pulls it out and dusts it off.* MAN *straightens, leaning forward eagerly.)*

A Bible. I didn't even know my dad had one of these. I'm not . . . I mean, I don't really know a lot about this stuff. Y'know what I've always thought was weird about Jesus? They nail 'im to a cross and all that, right? But the whole time He's dying, He knows He's gonna come back. The Easter thing, right? So, I mean, so what? Lots of people've died and didn't know if they were coming back, so as far as I can tell, He had it easy. *(Puts the Bible down and continues digging through the box)* It's gotta be here somewhere—

(He pulls out a metal cash box and starts working on the lock.)

It's hard for me, 'cuz I don't know if I'm comin' back. Or what I'm going towards. I just know something's gotta change. And it's up to me to change it.

(He flings the metal box open. He stops. Then stares inside. He looks up with big scared eyes . . . right at the MAN.)

I'm not a whiner, like I said. I know life's been kinda hard already. I've heard some people say it only gets harder.

(He looks in box, swallows. Reaches in and pulls out a handgun. The MAN *jumps up and walks over to* BRIAN.)

Before I do this, I wish I knew. Can anybody tell me? What's after this? Is this permanent? Is there any comin' back? I wish my dad could come back. I wish he could come back like Jesus and tell me.

(The MAN *stands behind* BRIAN, *and puts his hand on his own head.)*

Reincarnation? Eternal damnation? Salvation?

*(*BRIAN*'s hand, holding the gun, starts to shake.)*

Somebody stop me.

(The MAN*'s hand shoots out, desperately reaching for the gun . . .)*

Blackout